Making Money Online:
The untold basics

By

Robertson J Peters

Table of contents

Chapter 1

Making money online can be a viable and rewarding endeavor, but it's important to approach it with realistic expectations. Here are some additional points to keep in mind:

1. Hard Work and Consistency: Just like any other form of income, making money online usually requires hard work and persistence. Success rarely comes overnight. Building a sustainable online income often involves putting in consistent effort over time.

2. Learning and Skill Development: Depending on the method you choose, you may need to acquire new skills or knowledge. Be prepared to invest time in learning and improving your abilities.

3. Market Research: Before starting any online venture, it's crucial to research your target market, competition, and potential profitability. Understanding

your niche and audience can significantly increase your chances of success.

4. Investment and Risk: Some online opportunities may require an initial investment, such as setting up a website or buying inventory for an online store. Be aware of the risks associated with these investments and only spend what you can afford to lose.

5. Diversification: Relying solely on one online income stream can be risky. Diversify your income sources to reduce vulnerability. For example, if you're a content creator, consider multiple platforms or revenue streams like affiliate marketing or merchandise sales.

6. Scams and Frauds: Be cautious of online scams and fraudulent schemes promising quick riches. If something sounds too good to be true, it probably is. Research any opportunity

thoroughly and be skeptical of get-rich-quick claims.

7. Legal and Tax Considerations: Depending on your location and the nature of your online income, there may be legal and tax implications to consider. Consult with professionals if necessary to ensure compliance.

8. Customer Trust: If you're selling products or services online, building trust with your audience is crucial. Delivering quality and value consistently will help you establish a positive reputation.

9. Adaptation: The online landscape is constantly evolving. What works today may not work as effectively tomorrow. Stay open to new ideas and be willing to adapt your strategies.

Here are the various ways one can make money online legitimately:
Freelancing:

Chapter 2

Freelancing is a popular and accessible way to make money online. Here are some steps to get started with freelancing on platforms like Upwork, Fiverr, or Freelancer:

1. Identify Your Skills: Determine what skills or services you can offer as a freelancer. This could be writing, graphic design, web development, social media management, translation, video editing, and more. Your skills should align with your interests and expertise.

2. Create a Portfolio: Building a portfolio is crucial for showcasing your work to potential clients. If you're a writer, compile writing samples; if you're a designer, showcase your design projects. Ensure your portfolio reflects your best work.

3. Choose the Right Platform: Research and choose a freelancing platform that suits your skills and goals. Some platforms are better for specific

niches, so pick one where your services are in demand. Sign up for an account and complete your profile with a professional photo and a well-written bio.

4. Set Competitive Rates: Determine your pricing strategy. Consider your experience, the complexity of the work, and market rates. Starting with competitive rates can help you attract initial clients.

5. Create Gig or Service Listings: On platforms like Fiverr, you'll create "gigs" or service listings. These should be clear, concise, and appealing to potential clients. Highlight what you offer and the value clients will receive.

6. Bid on Jobs: On platforms like Upwork and Freelancer, you'll bid on job postings. Craft personalized proposals that address the client's needs, showcase your relevant skills, and explain why you're the best fit for the job.

7. Deliver High-Quality Work: Once you land a project, focus on delivering top-notch work within the agreed-upon timeframe. Satisfied clients are more likely to leave positive reviews and hire you for future projects.

8. Build Your Reputation: Positive reviews and ratings are crucial in the freelancing world. Consistently provide excellent service, meet deadlines, and communicate effectively with clients to build a strong reputation.

9. Expand Your Skills: Continuously improve your skills to stay competitive. Online courses, workshops, and tutorials can help you stay up-to-date in your field.

10. Network: Networking can be valuable in freelancing. Connect with other freelancers in your niche, join online communities, and attend

webinars or conferences related to
your field.

11. Manage Finances: Keep track of your
income and expenses, and set aside
money for taxes. Freelancers often
have to handle their own taxes and
financial planning.

12. Plan for Growth: As you gain
experience and positive reviews,
consider expanding your freelancing
business. You might increase your
rates, add new services, or target
higher-paying clients.

Remember that freelancing success may
take time to achieve. It's essential to be
patient, persistent, and professional in your
interactions with clients. Over time, you can
build a rewarding freelancing career and
potentially earn a substantial income online.

Chapter 3

Online Content Creation:

Creating online content is a fantastic way to express yourself, share your expertise, and potentially earn money. Whether you want to start a YouTube channel, TikTok account, or a blog, here are steps to help you get started with online content creation:

1. Choose Your Niche: Select a niche or topic that you're passionate about and have knowledge or interest in. Your enthusiasm will come through in your content and make it more engaging.

2. Research Your Audience: Understand your target audience. What are their interests, problems, and questions? Tailor your content to meet their needs and preferences.

3. Platform Selection: Depending on your content type, choose the appropriate platform(s). For longer-form videos or articles, consider YouTube or blogging. For short videos and quick engagement, TikTok or Instagram Reels may be ideal.

4. Create High-Quality Content: Invest in good equipment, whether it's a camera, microphone, or editing software. High-quality content is more likely to attract and retain viewers.

5. Plan Your Content: Create a content calendar to schedule your posts and maintain consistency. Consistency is key to building an audience.

6. Optimize for SEO: For blogs and YouTube, learn about search engine optimization (SEO) to increase the visibility of your content in search results.

7. Engage with Your Audience: Respond to comments, messages, and engage with your audience on social media. Building a community around your content is essential.

8. Monetization Strategies: To earn money, explore various monetization methods:

   - Ad Revenue: On platforms like YouTube, you can earn money

through ads displayed on your videos.

- Sponsorships: Brands may pay you to promote their products or services if you have a substantial following.
- Affiliate Marketing: Promote products or services and earn a commission on sales generated through your unique affiliate links.
- Merchandise Sales: If you have a dedicated audience, consider selling merchandise related to your content.
- Paid Memberships: Platforms like Patreon allow you to offer exclusive content to paying subscribers.
- Donations and Crowdfunding: Some content creators rely on donations from their audience through platforms like PayPal,

Venmo, or crowdfunding sites like Kickstarter or Indiegogo.

9. Build a Brand: Develop a consistent brand identity, including a logo, color scheme, and style that reflects your content and personality.

10. Track and Analyze: Use analytics tools provided by the platform or third-party tools to track the performance of your content. This helps you understand what works and what doesn't.

11. Stay Updated: The online content landscape is ever-evolving. Stay updated on trends and changes in algorithms to adapt your content strategy.

12. Be Patient: Building an audience and earning substantial income through online content takes time. Don't be discouraged by slow growth at the beginning.

Remember that your content should provide value to your audience. Authenticity, passion, and a genuine desire to help or entertain others are key ingredients for success in online content creation.

Chapter 4

eCommerce:
Starting an eCommerce business can be a lucrative way to make money online. Here are steps to get started with your own online store:

1. Choose Your Niche: Decide on the niche or market you want to target. Consider your interests, expertise, and the demand for products in that niche. Research your competition to identify opportunities.
2. Market Research: Research your target audience and their preferences. Identify their pain points, needs, and buying behavior. This information will help you select products and create marketing strategies.

3. Select Your Business Model:
    - Dropshipping: Partner with suppliers who will fulfill orders on your behalf. You won't need to hold inventory, but you'll have less control over shipping and product quality.
    - Inventory-based eCommerce: Purchase and manage your own inventory. This provides more control over product quality and shipping but requires more upfront investment.
    - Digital Products: Sell downloadable products like eBooks, software, online courses, or digital artwork.
4. Choose a Platform: Select an eCommerce platform to build your online store. Popular options include:
    - Shopify: A user-friendly platform with a range of features and templates.

- WooCommerce: A plugin for WordPress, ideal for those who want to integrate an online store with their blog or website.
- BigCommerce: Known for its scalability and built-in features.
- Amazon and eBay: You can also sell products on established marketplaces, but be aware of the fees associated with these platforms.

5. Domain Name and Hosting: Register a domain name that reflects your brand and choose a hosting provider that supports your eCommerce platform.

6. Design Your Online Store: Customize the design of your online store, focusing on a user-friendly layout, clear product descriptions, high-quality images, and an easy checkout process.

7. Set Up Payment and Shipping: Configure payment gateways (e.g., PayPal, Stripe) and establish shipping

methods and rates. Consider offering free shipping or competitive rates to attract customers.

8. Add Products: Populate your store with products, including detailed descriptions, prices, and high-resolution images. Organize products into categories for easy navigation.

9. Optimize for SEO: Implement on-page SEO techniques to improve your store's visibility in search engines. Use relevant keywords in product titles, descriptions, and meta tags.

10. Create a Marketing Plan: Develop a marketing strategy to attract customers. This may include social media marketing, email marketing, content marketing, pay-per-click advertising, and search engine optimization.

11. Launch Your Store: Test your store thoroughly, ensuring that all links, buttons, and payment processes work

correctly. Make a soft launch to friends and family to gather feedback, then officially launch your store.

12. Monitor and Analyze: Use analytics tools to track website traffic, sales, and customer behavior. Adjust your marketing strategies based on data insights.

13. Customer Support: Provide excellent customer support to address inquiries, issues, and returns promptly. Good customer service can lead to repeat business and positive reviews.

14. Scale Your Business: As your store grows, consider expanding your product range, improving customer experience, and exploring additional marketing channels.

Remember that eCommerce success takes time and effort. Building trust with customers and providing a positive shopping experience are key to long-term success in the online retail space.

Chapter 5

Online Surveys and Market Research: Participating in online surveys and market research can be a simple way to earn some extra money or gift cards by sharing your opinions. Here's how to get started:

1. Research Survey Platforms: Start by researching and identifying reputable online survey and market research platforms. Some popular ones include Swagbucks, Survey Junkie, Amazon Mechanical Turk (MTurk), Pinecone Research, and Vindale Research. Read reviews and user experiences to ensure they are legitimate and trustworthy.

2. Create Accounts: Sign up for accounts on the platforms you've chosen. You may need to provide some basic information about yourself during the registration process.

3. Complete Your Profile: After signing up, complete your profile on each platform. This information helps survey providers match you with relevant surveys.

4. Explore Available Surveys: Once your profile is set up, you'll typically find a list of available surveys or tasks. Some surveys may have specific qualifications or requirements, so read the details carefully.

5. Take Surveys: Participate in surveys that match your demographics and interests. Surveys can vary in length and complexity, and the compensation usually reflects this. Be honest and provide thoughtful responses to survey questions.

6. Earn Rewards: Depending on the platform, you can earn cash, gift cards, points, or other rewards for completing surveys. Check the redemption options and choose the one that suits you best.

7. Set Realistic Expectations: While participating in online surveys can be a way to earn some extra money or rewards, it's not a get-rich-quick scheme. The income is typically modest, and it may take time to accumulate enough rewards to cash out.

8. Stay Consistent: Consistency is key to maximizing your earnings. Log in regularly to check for new surveys and opportunities.

9. Refer Friends: Some survey platforms offer referral programs where you can earn additional rewards for referring friends or family members to join.

10. Protect Your Information: Be cautious about sharing sensitive information. Legitimate survey platforms will not ask for your financial details, such as bank account numbers or Social Security numbers.

11. Avoid Scams: Be wary of survey offers that promise huge rewards for little

effort. Scams exist in the online survey space, so if something seems too good to be true, it probably is.
12. Diversify Your Income Sources: Consider combining online surveys with other online income streams to increase your overall earnings.

Remember that online surveys are not a primary source of income for most people, but they can be a convenient way to earn some extra cash or gift cards in your spare time. Always use trusted and reputable platforms to ensure your safety and security while participating in online surveys and market research.

Chapter 6

Remote Work:
Remote work has become increasingly popular, and many companies now offer opportunities for employees to work from

home or from anywhere in the world. Here's how you can find remote job listings and increase your chances of securing a remote position:

1. Update Your Resume and LinkedIn Profile: Before you start your job search, make sure your resume and LinkedIn profile highlight your relevant skills and experience. Mention any past remote work experience if applicable.

2. Identify Your Skills: Determine what skills and qualifications you have that are suitable for remote work. Many remote jobs require strong communication skills, self-discipline, and the ability to work independently.

3. Choose Job Search Websites: Use reputable job search websites that specialize in remote job listings. Some popular options include:

   - Remote.co: This platform focuses exclusively on remote job opportunities.

- We Work Remotely: A job board
  with a wide range of remote job
  listings.
- FlexJobs: Known for its curated
  listings of flexible and remote
  jobs.
- LinkedIn: Use LinkedIn's job
  search filters to find remote job
  postings. You can also join
  LinkedIn groups dedicated to
  remote work opportunities.

4. Use Keywords: When searching for
   remote jobs, use specific keywords like
   "remote," "telecommute," "work from
   home," or "virtual" in your search
   queries. This helps filter out on-site
   positions.
5. Set Up Job Alerts: Most job search
   websites allow you to set up job alerts
   based on your preferences. Receive
   email notifications when new remote
   job listings that match your criteria
   become available.

6. Network: Leverage your professional network to inquire about remote job opportunities. Connect with people who work remotely or in your desired industry on LinkedIn.

7. Customize Your Cover Letter: Tailor your cover letter for each remote job application, emphasizing your remote work skills and explaining why you're a good fit for a remote position.

8. Prepare for Remote Interviews: Remote job interviews may include video calls or other remote communication methods. Familiarize yourself with the technology and be prepared for virtual interviews.

9. Research Companies: Before applying, research the companies you're interested in. Consider their culture, reputation, and reviews from current or former employees.

10. Be Patient and Persistent: Landing a remote job may take time, especially if you're just starting your remote

work journey. Stay persistent and keep applying to positions that match your skills and interests.

11. Consider Freelancing or Contract Work: If you're struggling to find a full-time remote job, consider freelance or contract work as an interim solution. Websites like Upwork and Fiverr offer freelance opportunities.

12. Expand Your Skill Set: Consider acquiring additional skills or certifications that are in demand for remote work positions. This can make you a more attractive candidate.

Remember that remote work comes with its unique challenges, such as self-discipline and effective communication. Be prepared to demonstrate your ability to manage these challenges during the application process and in your remote work role.

Affiliate Marketing:

Chapter 7

Affiliate marketing is a popular way to make money online by promoting products or services from other companies and earning a commission for each successful sale or lead. Here's how to get started with affiliate marketing:

1. Choose a Niche: Select a niche or industry that aligns with your interests or expertise. This will make it easier to create content and promote relevant products.

2. Build an Online Platform: You'll need a platform to promote affiliate products. This could be a website, blog, YouTube channel, social media profiles, or an email list. Your platform should have an audience interested in your chosen niche.

3. Select Affiliate Programs: Research and join affiliate programs that offer products or services related to your niche. There are many affiliate networks and individual company

programs to choose from. Popular affiliate networks include Amazon Associates, ClickBank, ShareASale, and CJ Affiliate.

4. Review and Choose Products: Within your selected affiliate programs, choose products or services to promote. Select products that you believe will genuinely benefit your audience. You can promote physical products, digital products, software, courses, and more.

5. Create High-Quality Content: Develop content that integrates affiliate product promotions naturally. This could be product reviews, tutorials, comparisons, or listicles. Ensure your content provides value to your audience.

6. Use Affiliate Links: Once you've selected products to promote, generate unique affiliate tracking links for each product. These links will track

referrals from your platform to the product's sales page.

7. Disclose Your Affiliate Relationship: It's crucial to be transparent with your audience. Clearly disclose that you may earn a commission if they make a purchase through your affiliate links. This builds trust with your audience.

8. Promote Strategically: Promote affiliate products within your content and marketing channels strategically. Avoid spammy or overly aggressive promotion methods. Focus on providing valuable information and solutions.

9. Track and Analyze Performance: Use tracking tools provided by the affiliate programs to monitor the performance of your affiliate links. Pay attention to clicks, conversions, and earnings. Analyze what's working and what's not.

10. Optimize Your Strategy: Based on your performance data, refine your

affiliate marketing strategy. Test different products, promotion methods, and content formats to optimize your earnings.

11. Diversify Income Streams: Consider joining multiple affiliate programs and promoting a variety of products to diversify your income sources. This can help you mitigate risks associated with changes in product availability or commission rates.

12. Comply with Regulations: Familiarize yourself with affiliate marketing regulations and guidelines in your region, such as the Federal Trade Commission (FTC) guidelines in the United States.

13. Stay Updated: The affiliate marketing landscape evolves, so stay updated on industry trends and changes. This will help you remain competitive and adapt your strategies accordingly.

Affiliate marketing can be a lucrative online income stream, but success often requires time, effort, and a deep understanding of your audience and chosen niche. Be patient and persistent, and continuously improve your affiliate marketing strategies to maximize your earnings.

Chapter 8

Online Teaching and Tutoring:
Online teaching and tutoring is a rewarding way to share your knowledge and expertise while earning money online. Whether you're a teacher, subject matter expert, or passionate about a particular topic, there are various platforms and approaches you can explore. Here's how to get started:

1. Identify Your Expertise: Determine the subject or skill you are proficient in and passionate about. This could be academic subjects, languages, music,

coding, art, or any area where you have knowledge to share.

2. Choose a Teaching Platform:
   - VIPKid: VIPKid primarily focuses on teaching English to students in China. It's a popular platform for English teachers.
   - Teachable: Teachable allows you to create and sell your own online courses. You have full control over the content, pricing, and branding.
   - Coursera: Coursera offers an opportunity to become an instructor and create courses within their platform, often in partnership with universities and institutions.
3. Meet Qualifications: Different platforms have various qualification requirements. For example, VIPKid may require a bachelor's degree and teaching experience, while Teachable allows anyone to create courses.

4. Create a Curriculum: If you're using platforms like Teachable or Coursera, develop a structured curriculum for your course or tutoring program. Plan lessons, assignments, and assessments.

5. Set Your Pricing: Decide how you'll charge for your teaching services. Some options include charging per lesson, per course enrollment, or on a subscription basis.

6. Create High-Quality Content: Whether you're teaching live or through pre-recorded lessons, focus on delivering high-quality content that engages and educates your students. Use multimedia, visuals, and interactive elements when appropriate.

7. Promote Your Services: If you're using platforms like Teachable or Coursera, you may need to promote your courses to attract students. Utilize social media, email marketing, and other

digital marketing strategies to reach your target audience.

8. Engage with Students: Interact with your students through discussions, Q&A sessions, or live office hours. Building a strong teacher-student relationship can enhance the learning experience.

9. Collect and Analyze Feedback: Encourage students to provide feedback, and use it to improve your teaching methods and content.

10. Stay Updated: Keep up with industry trends and educational best practices to ensure your teaching materials and methods remain relevant.

11. Manage Your Schedule: Create a teaching schedule that aligns with your availability and time zone. Be punctual and reliable for live teaching sessions.

12. Comply with Regulations: If you're teaching specific subjects or to specific

audiences, be aware of any legal or regulatory requirements that may apply to your online teaching activities.

13. Continuous Learning: Just like your students, continue learning and improving your skills. Consider taking courses or attending workshops to enhance your teaching abilities.

Online teaching and tutoring offer flexibility and the opportunity to reach a global audience. Whether you're looking to supplement your income or make teaching your full-time career, it's essential to provide quality education and continually adapt to the needs of your students.

Chapter 9

Stock Trading and Investment:
Investing in stocks, cryptocurrencies, or other financial instruments can potentially

grow your wealth over time, but it comes
with risks. Here are steps to consider when
getting involved in trading or investment:

1. Educate Yourself: Before you start
   investing, take the time to learn about
   the financial markets, different asset
   classes (stocks, bonds,
   cryptocurrencies, etc.), and various
   investment strategies. Understanding
   the basics is crucial for making
   informed decisions.

2. Set Clear Goals: Determine your
   investment objectives. Are you looking
   for short-term gains or long-term
   wealth accumulation? Your goals will
   influence your investment strategy.

3. Create a Budget: Establish a budget
   for your investments. Only invest
   money you can afford to lose. Never
   use money that you need for essential
   expenses like rent or bills.

4. Diversify Your Portfolio:
   Diversification is a key risk
   management strategy. Don't put all

your money into a single asset or type of investment. Spread your investments across different assets to reduce risk.

5. Choose a Brokerage Account: Open a brokerage account with a reputable and regulated brokerage firm. Consider factors like fees, user-friendliness, research tools, and the variety of assets available when selecting a platform.

6. Research Investments: Thoroughly research the assets you're interested in. Analyze financial statements, market trends, and the potential risks and rewards associated with each investment.

7. Start Small: If you're new to investing, consider starting with a small amount of money. This allows you to gain experience without exposing yourself to significant risk.

8. Practice with Virtual Accounts: Some brokerage platforms offer virtual

trading accounts with virtual money. Use these to practice your trading strategies without risking real capital.

9. Create an Investment Strategy: Develop a clear investment strategy that aligns with your goals and risk tolerance. Consider strategies like value investing, growth investing, or dollar-cost averaging.

10. Stay Informed: Stay updated on financial news, economic events, and market developments that may impact your investments. Knowledge is essential for making informed decisions.

11. Monitor Your Investments: Regularly review your portfolio and make adjustments as needed. Rebalance your portfolio to maintain your desired asset allocation.

12. Avoid Emotional Decisions: Emotions can lead to impulsive decisions that may harm your investment performance. Stick to your strategy

and avoid making knee-jerk reactions to market fluctuations.

13. Understand Risk: All investments carry some level of risk. Understand the risks associated with each investment and be prepared for the possibility of losses.

14. Consider Professional Advice: If you're unsure about your investment choices or need personalized guidance, consider consulting with a financial advisor.

15. Long-Term Perspective: Successful investing often requires a long-term perspective. Avoid trying to time the market or chase short-term gains.

16. Stay Patient: Investments can fluctuate in value, and it's common to experience periods of both gains and losses. Patience is key to successful investing.

Remember that investing involves inherent risks, and there are no guarantees of profits. Be cautious, do your research, and make informed decisions based on your financial goals and risk tolerance. If in doubt, seek advice from a financial professional.

Chapter 10

Remote Freelance Writing:
Remote freelance writing is a flexible and accessible way to make money online if you have strong writing skills. Here are steps to help you get started with freelance writing:

Assess Your Writing Skills: Before diving in, assess your writing skills objectively. Consider your strengths and areas for improvement. Effective freelance writers have good grammar, punctuation, and the ability to write clearly and concisely.

Choose Your Niche: Determine your writing niche or areas of expertise. Freelance writers can specialize in a wide range of topics, such as technology, health, travel, finance, lifestyle, and more. Specializing in a niche can help you stand out and attract clients interested in your expertise.

Build a Portfolio: Create a portfolio that showcases your writing skills. Include a variety of writing samples in your chosen niche. If you don't have published work, consider writing sample articles or blog posts to demonstrate your abilities.

Set Your Rates: Decide on your freelance writing rates. Rates can vary widely depending on factors like your experience, expertise, and the complexity of the writing projects. Research industry standards and adjust your rates accordingly.

Create a Professional Online Presence: Build an online presence that reflects your professionalism as a freelance writer. Create a professional website or blog where potential clients can learn more about your services and view your portfolio.

Use Freelance Marketplaces: Join freelancing platforms like Upwork, Fiverr, Freelancer, or Guru. These platforms connect freelancers with clients looking for writing services. Create a compelling profile that highlights your skills and experiences.

Apply for Jobs: Browse job listings on freelance marketplaces and apply to writing gigs that match your skills and interests. Craft personalized proposals for each job application, explaining why you're a suitable candidate.

Network: Networking can be valuable in the freelance writing industry. Connect with other freelance writers, join writing communities or forums, and attend writing-related events or webinars.

Deliver High-Quality Work: When you secure freelance writing projects, focus on delivering high-quality work that meets the client's requirements. Be professional, meet deadlines, and maintain open communication with clients.

Ask for Feedback: After completing a project, request feedback from clients. Positive reviews and testimonials can enhance your reputation as a freelance writer.

Expand Your Skills: Continuously improve your writing skills and stay updated on industry trends. Consider taking writing courses or workshops to enhance your abilities.

Manage Your Finances: Keep track of your income and expenses as a freelancer. Consider setting aside money for taxes and consider budgeting for periods with irregular income.

Seek Repeat Clients: Building long-term relationships with clients can lead to a steady stream of work. If a client is satisfied with your work, ask if they have additional writing needs. Protect Your Work: Be aware of copyright and ownership issues. Ensure you have a clear agreement with clients regarding who owns the rights to the content you create.

Freelance writing can be a rewarding career path, offering flexibility and the opportunity to work on a variety of projects. However, it may take time to establish yourself and build a steady stream of clients. Be persistent and continually work on improving your writing skills and marketing efforts to succeed in the freelance writing industry.

Chapter 11

Online Coaching or Consulting:
Offering online coaching or consulting services can be a lucrative way to share your

expertise and earn money online. Whether you're knowledgeable in a specific field or have valuable insights to offer, here are steps to get started:

1. Identify Your Expertise: Determine the subject or area in which you have expertise and can provide valuable guidance. This could be related to business, career development, fitness, nutrition, life coaching, marketing, or any other field.
2. Define Your Niche: Narrow down your expertise to a specific niche within your chosen field. Specializing in a niche can help you attract a more targeted audience.
3. Set Clear Goals: Establish clear objectives for your coaching or consulting business. Decide on your income goals, the number of clients you want to work with, and the types of services you'll offer.
4. Create a Brand: Develop a professional brand identity for your

coaching or consulting services. This includes creating a professional website, logo, and branding materials that reflect your expertise.

5. Build an Online Presence: Establish a strong online presence through a website, blog, or social media profiles. Share valuable content related to your niche to showcase your knowledge.

6. Choose a Platform: Decide whether you want to offer coaching or consulting services independently through your website or through a platform that connects experts with clients, such as Clarity.fm, Coach.me, or even video conferencing platforms like Zoom or Skype.

7. Set Your Rates: Determine your pricing structure for coaching or consulting sessions. Research industry standards and consider your level of expertise when setting rates.

8. Create Service Packages: Develop service packages that outline what

clients can expect from your coaching or consulting sessions. Clearly define the benefits and outcomes clients can achieve through your services.

9. Market Your Services: Promote your coaching or consulting services through various marketing channels. Utilize social media, content marketing, email marketing, and networking to reach potential clients.

10.   Offer Free Consultations: To attract clients, consider offering free initial consultations. This allows potential clients to experience your services and decide if they want to work with you.

11. Provide Exceptional Service: Deliver high-quality coaching or consulting sessions tailored to each client's needs. Focus on helping clients achieve their goals and provide value during each interaction.

12. Collect Testimonials and Reviews: Encourage satisfied clients to leave testimonials or reviews on your

website or platform profiles. Positive feedback can boost your credibility.

13. Stay Updated: Continuously update your knowledge and skills in your chosen field. Stay informed about industry trends and best practices to offer the most up-to-date guidance.

14. Network: Build relationships with other professionals in your industry, attend virtual conferences, and join relevant online communities to expand your network.

15. Manage Your Schedule: Efficiently manage your coaching or consulting schedule to accommodate client sessions and maintain a work-life balance.

16. Comply with Regulations: Depending on your industry and location, there may be regulations or certifications required for offering coaching or consulting services. Ensure you comply with any legal requirements.

Online coaching and consulting can provide a fulfilling way to share your expertise, help others achieve their goals, and earn income online. Success in this field often comes from a combination of your expertise, effective marketing, and exceptional client service.

Chapter 12

Sell Photography or Art:
Selling your photography or art online can be a great way to showcase your creativity and potentially earn income. Here's how to get started:

1. Select Your Best Work: Choose a selection of your best photographs or artworks to showcase. Quality matters, so focus on pieces that demonstrate your skills and artistic vision.
2. Prepare Your Artwork: Ensure your images are of high resolution and quality. If you're selling physical art,

photograph it under good lighting conditions to capture the details accurately.

3. Choose an Online Platform:
    - Shutterstock, Adobe Stock, or iStock: These platforms are ideal for selling stock photos and illustrations. You can upload your work and earn royalties when customers purchase and use your images.
    - Etsy: If you create handmade art, crafts, or prints, Etsy is a popular marketplace for selling your physical and digital artwork.
    - Redbubble and Society6: These platforms are great for artists and photographers looking to sell their work on various products like prints, clothing, phone cases, and more.
4. Create an Account: Sign up for an account on the platform(s) you've

chosen. Complete your profile and provide accurate and engaging information about yourself and your artwork.

5. Upload Your Art: Follow the platform's guidelines for uploading your artwork. Provide detailed descriptions, tags, and pricing information for each piece.

6. Set Pricing: Research similar artwork and price your work competitively. Consider factors like size, complexity, and demand when determining your pricing strategy.

7. Optimize for Search: Use relevant keywords in your titles, descriptions, and tags to improve the visibility of your artwork in search results.

8. Provide High-Quality Images: Ensure that your product images accurately represent your artwork. High-resolution photos and multiple angles can help buyers make informed decisions.

9. Promote Your Shop: Promote your shop and artwork through social media, your website or blog, email newsletters, and online art communities. Building an audience can help attract buyers to your shop.

10. Engage with Customers: Respond promptly to inquiries, provide excellent customer service, and engage with customers through comments, reviews, and messages.

11. Offer Variety: Consider offering a variety of products with your artwork, such as prints, canvas prints, framed art, posters, or merchandise like T-shirts and mugs.

12. Fulfill Orders Promptly: If you're selling physical products, ship them promptly and securely. Provide tracking information and communicate with customers about the status of their orders.

13. Protect Your Work: Be aware of copyright and intellectual property

issues. If you're selling art that includes recognizable trademarks or copyrighted material, ensure you have the necessary permissions.

14. Stay Updated: Continuously update your shop with new artwork to keep it fresh and attract repeat customers.
15. Manage Finances: Keep track of your income and expenses related to your art sales. Be prepared to handle taxes on your earnings.

Selling your photography or art online requires both creative talent and business acumen. Success may take time, so be patient and persistent. By consistently producing high-quality work and effectively marketing it to the right audience, you can build a successful online art business.

Chapter 13

Dropshipping:

Dropshipping is an eCommerce business model that allows you to sell products online without holding inventory. Here's a step-by-step guide on how to start a dropshipping business:

1. Choose a Niche: Select a niche or product category that interests you and has a demand in the market. Consider factors like competition, profit margins, and trends when making your choice.

2. Market Research: Research your target audience, including their preferences, pain points, and buying behavior. Understand your competitors and identify opportunities to differentiate your store.

3. Create a Business Plan: Develop a business plan that outlines your business goals, budget, and marketing strategy. Consider your pricing strategy and how you'll attract customers.

4. Legal and Business Setup:

- Register Your Business: Depending on your location, you may need to register your business and obtain any necessary licenses or permits.
- Choose a Business Name: Select a unique and memorable name for your dropshipping store.
- Set Up a Business Bank Account: Keep your business finances separate from personal finances by opening a dedicated business bank account.

5. Select Products to Sell:
- Find Reliable Suppliers: Research and partner with reputable suppliers who offer dropshipping services. Some popular options include AliExpress, SaleHoo, and Oberlo (for Shopify stores).
- Product Selection: Choose products that fit your niche and have a good track record of

sales. Consider factors like product quality, shipping times, and supplier reliability.

6. Set Up an Online Store:
    - Choose an eCommerce Platform: Select an eCommerce platform to build your online store. Shopify, WooCommerce, and BigCommerce are popular options.
    - Design Your Store: Customize your store's appearance, including the theme, logo, and layout. Ensure it's user-friendly and mobile-responsive.
    - Set Up Payment and Shipping: Configure payment gateways (e.g., PayPal, Stripe) and establish shipping methods and rates. Consider offering free shipping or competitive rates to attract customers.

7. Import Products: Use your chosen eCommerce platform and any

necessary plugins to import products from your suppliers to your online store. Ensure that product details, descriptions, and images are accurate and attractive.

8. Optimize for SEO: Implement search engine optimization (SEO) strategies to improve your store's visibility in search engine results. Use relevant keywords in product titles and descriptions.

9. Create Content: Write product descriptions, blog posts, and other content that engages and educates your audience. High-quality content can help drive organic traffic to your site.

10. Marketing and Promotion:
    - Social Media Marketing: Utilize social media platforms to promote your products and engage with your audience.
    - Email Marketing: Build an email list and send newsletters to

subscribers with special offers
and product updates.

- Paid Advertising: Consider using
  paid advertising channels like
  Google Ads, Facebook Ads, or
  Instagram Ads to drive traffic to
  your store.

11. Customer Service: Provide excellent
customer support, including
responding to inquiries promptly,
addressing concerns, and processing
returns and refunds efficiently.

12. Analyze and Optimize: Use analytics
tools to track the performance of your
products and marketing efforts. Make
data-driven decisions to optimize your
store and increase conversions.

13. Scale Your Business: As your
dropshipping business grows,
consider expanding your product
offerings, diversifying suppliers, and
exploring new marketing channels.

Dropshipping can be a profitable online business, but success requires careful planning, effective marketing, and excellent customer service. Be prepared for challenges like competition and fluctuating product availability. Continuous learning and adaptability are essential for long-term success in the dropshipping industry.

Chapter 14

App or Software Development:
Creating and selling mobile apps or software programs can be a rewarding way to leverage your programming skills and generate income. Here's a step-by-step guide to get you started in app or software development:

1. Identify a Niche or Problem: Start by identifying a specific niche or a problem that your app or software can address. Conduct market research to

understand your target audience and their needs.

2. Plan Your App or Software:
   - Define the core features and functionality of your app or software.
   - Create wireframes or prototypes to visualize the user interface and user experience.
   - Develop a comprehensive project plan with timelines and milestones.
3. Choose a Development Platform: Decide whether you want to create mobile apps (iOS and Android) or desktop software (Windows, macOS, Linux), or both. Select the appropriate development tools and programming languages based on your target platforms.
4. Learn or Hire Development Skills: If you don't already possess the necessary development skills, consider learning or hiring a developer. You

can use online courses, tutorials, and resources to build your programming knowledge.

5. Build Your App or Software:
   - Write code to develop your app or software based on your project plan.
   - Test your app or software thoroughly to identify and fix any bugs or issues.
   - Iterate on your project to improve functionality and user experience.

6. Design the User Interface (UI): Create an intuitive and visually appealing user interface for your app or software. Good design enhances the user experience and increases the chances of success.

7. Monetization Strategy: Determine how you'll make money from your app or software. Common monetization strategies include selling the app or software, offering a free version with

in-app purchases or ads, or using a
subscription model.

8. Set Pricing: If you plan to sell your app
   or software, research competitors and
   similar products to set a competitive
   price. Consider factors like the value
   you offer, target audience, and market
   demand.

9. Create a Website or Landing Page:
   Build a website or landing page to
   promote your app or software. Include
   information about its features,
   benefits, pricing, and a call to action
   for users to download or purchase.

10. Marketing and Promotion:
    - Utilize digital marketing
      channels such as social media,
      content marketing, email
      marketing, and paid advertising
      to promote your app or software.
    - Reach out to potential users,
      influencers, or industry blogs for
      reviews and features.

- Leverage app stores like Apple's App Store or Google Play for mobile apps to increase discoverability.

11. Provide Customer Support: Offer excellent customer support to address user inquiries, feedback, and technical issues. Engage with your user community to build trust and improve your product.

12. Collect User Feedback: Continuously gather feedback from users to identify areas for improvement and new features to add.

13. Update and Maintain: Regularly update your app or software to fix bugs, add new features, and ensure compatibility with the latest operating systems or platforms.

14. Protect Intellectual Property: Consider copyright or trademark protection for your app or software, especially if it includes unique branding or features.

15. Monitor Performance: Use analytics tools to track user engagement, retention, and other key performance metrics. Adjust your strategy based on data insights.
16. Scale and Expand: As your app or software gains popularity, consider expanding to other platforms or markets and exploring partnerships or collaborations.

Remember that successful app or software development requires dedication, ongoing improvement, and a clear understanding of your target audience. It may take time to build a user base and generate significant income, so be patient and persistent in your efforts.

Chapter 15

Virtual Assistance:

Starting a virtual assistant business can be a lucrative way to offer administrative, customer service, or support services to businesses remotely. Here's a step-by-step guide to help you get started:

1. Identify Your Skills and Services:
   - Determine the skills and services you can offer as a virtual assistant. These may include administrative tasks, data entry, email management, social media management, customer support, bookkeeping, and more.
2. Choose Your Niche:
   - Consider specializing in a specific niche or industry, such as real estate, healthcare, e-commerce, or digital marketing. Specialization can help you stand out and target a specific audience.
3. Set Up Your Home Office:
   - Create a dedicated workspace in your home with the necessary

equipment, including a computer, high-speed internet, phone, and any software tools or applications relevant to your services.

4. Business Registration and Licensing:
   - Depending on your location and local regulations, you may need to register your virtual assistance business, obtain any required licenses, and check tax obligations.

5. Create a Business Plan:
   - Develop a business plan outlining your services, target market, pricing structure, marketing strategy, and financial projections. A business plan will help you stay organized and focused.

6. Pricing Your Services:
   - Research industry standards and competitor rates to determine how much to charge for your

services. Consider factors like your experience and the complexity of tasks.

7. Build an Online Presence:
    - Create a professional website that showcases your services, portfolio, client testimonials, and contact information. Your website is your online business card.
    - Set up profiles on professional networking platforms like LinkedIn and social media channels relevant to your niche.

8. Marketing and Networking:
    - Develop a marketing strategy to attract clients. Utilize online marketing methods, including content marketing, email marketing, social media marketing, and paid advertising.
    - Network with other virtual assistants, entrepreneurs, and potential clients in your niche.

Join industry-specific groups and forums to build relationships.

9. Legal Contracts and Agreements:
    - Draft clear and comprehensive service agreements or contracts to protect both you and your clients. Outline services, terms, payment terms, confidentiality, and dispute resolution procedures.

10. Client Onboarding:
    - Develop an onboarding process for new clients. This may include a consultation, discussing their needs, setting expectations, and clarifying your workflow.

11. Time Management and Organization:
    - Implement effective time management and organization tools, such as calendars, task lists, project management software, and virtual assistants for yourself.

12. Customer Service and Communication:
   - Provide excellent customer service by responding promptly to inquiries, communicating clearly, and maintaining professionalism in all interactions.
13. Payment and Invoicing:
   - Set up a reliable invoicing and payment system. Consider using online payment platforms to streamline the process.
14. Continual Learning:
   - Stay updated on industry trends, tools, and software applications to enhance your skills and offer better services to your clients.
15. Client Retention and Growth:
   - Focus on building long-term relationships with clients. Satisfied clients are more likely to provide repeat business and referrals.

16. Scale Your Business:

- As your business grows, consider hiring additional virtual assistants or expanding your service offerings to meet client demand.

Starting a virtual assistant business requires determination, organization, and effective communication skills. By providing valuable services and building strong client relationships, you can create a successful and sustainable virtual assistance business.

Chapter 16

Online Courses and eBooks:
Creating and selling online courses or eBooks can be a profitable venture, whether you're an expert in a particular field or have valuable knowledge to share. Here's a step-by-step guide to help you get started:

☐ Creating and Selling Online Courses:

- Choose Your Course Topic: Select a niche or subject you're passionate about and have expertise in. Ensure there's a demand for the topic by conducting market research.
- Plan Your Course:
    a. Outline the course structure, including modules, lessons, and objectives.
    b. Determine the format (video, text, quizzes, assignments) and the length of each lesson.
    c. Create a syllabus or curriculum that guides the learning journey.
- Content Creation:
    a. Develop high-quality course content, such as video lectures, written materials, quizzes, and assignments.
    b. Use appropriate tools and software for content creation, like video recording/editing software or eLearning authoring tools.

- Set Up a Learning Platform:
    a. Choose a platform to host your online course. Popular options include Udemy, Teachable, Thinkific, and Kajabi.
    b. Customize your course landing page and include a compelling course description, pricing details, and instructor bio.
- Pricing and Monetization:
    a. Decide on your course pricing strategy. Consider factors like course quality, competition, and your target audience's budget.
    b. Offer free previews or sample lessons to attract potential students.
- Market Your Course:
    a. Develop a marketing strategy to promote your course. Utilize social media, email marketing, content marketing, and paid advertising.

    b. Leverage your existing online presence, such as a blog or social media following, to attract students.

- Engage with Students:
    a. Interact with your students through discussion forums, Q&A sessions, and email communication.
    b. Provide timely responses to student queries and feedback.
- Collect and Analyze Feedback:
    a. Encourage students to provide feedback on your course. Use their input to improve and enhance the learning experience.
- Scale Your Course Business:
    a. Consider creating additional courses in your niche or expanding into related topics.
    b. Offer discounts, bundles, or subscription models to attract more students.

☐ Creating and Selling eBooks:
Choose Your eBook Topic: Select a subject or genre for your eBook. Ensure it's a topic that interests you and has a potential audience.
Write and Edit Your eBook:

- Write your eBook content, ensuring it's well-researched, well-organized, and free from errors.
- Edit and proofread your eBook carefully or consider hiring a professional editor.

Design Your eBook:

- Create an attractive eBook cover that entices readers. Consider hiring a professional designer if you're not skilled in graphic design.
- Format your eBook for various eBook readers, such as Kindle, ePub, and PDF.

Publish Your eBook:

- Choose a publishing platform like Amazon Kindle Direct Publishing (KDP), Apple Books, Smashwords, or Draft2Digital.
- Follow the platform's guidelines for uploading your eBook, setting pricing, and choosing distribution options.

Set eBook Pricing:

- Research similar eBooks and set a competitive price based on factors like book length and genre.
- Consider offering a limited-time promotional price or free giveaways to attract readers.

Market Your eBook:

- Develop a marketing plan to promote your eBook. Utilize social media, author websites, email newsletters, and book promotion sites.

- Seek reviews from book bloggers or websites related to your genre.

Engage with Readers:
- Interact with readers through social media, author websites, or book forums.
- Encourage readers to leave reviews and share their feedback.

Monitor Sales and Reviews:
- Keep track of eBook sales and monitor reader reviews. Use this feedback to make improvements in future eBooks.

Write More eBooks:
- Consider writing and publishing more eBooks to build your author brand and expand your reader base.

Remember that success in creating and selling online courses or eBooks often requires persistence, marketing effort, and continuous improvement based on reader or student feedback. Over time, as you build a reputation and grow your audience, your earnings can increase.

Summary

Making money online, like any other endeavor, requires diligence and a cautious approach. Here are a few additional tips to keep in mind:

1. Avoid Get-Rich-Quick Schemes: Be skeptical of any opportunity that promises overnight wealth with minimal effort. If it sounds too good to be true, it probably is.
2. Do Thorough Research: Before investing time or money in any online opportunity, research it extensively. Look for reviews, testimonials, and user experiences from credible sources.

3. Protect Your Personal Information: Be cautious about sharing personal or financial information online, especially with unfamiliar websites or individuals.

4. Learn Continuously: Stay updated on the latest trends and developments in the online money-making space. The digital landscape evolves rapidly, and staying informed can help you adapt and succeed.

5. Diversify Income Streams: Relying on a single method to make money online can be risky. Consider diversifying your income sources to reduce dependence on one platform or strategy.

6. Build Trust and Credibility: Whether you're selling products, offering services, or creating content, building trust with your audience is essential. Be honest, transparent, and provide value to your customers or audience.

7. Seek Professional Advice: If you're unsure about any financial or legal aspects of your online business, consider consulting with a financial advisor or legal expert.

8. Stay Persistent: Success in making money online often doesn't happen overnight. It may take time to build a sustainable income stream.

9. Manage Your Finances: Keep track of your online earnings and expenses. Budget wisely and set aside funds for taxes if applicable.

10. Network and Collaborate: Building relationships and collaborating with others in your niche or industry can open up new opportunities and insights.

Remember that while there are legitimate and profitable ways to make money online, there are also scams and fraudulent schemes. Being cautious and well-informed

is your best defense against online scams
and a key to long-term success.

www.ingramcontent.com/pod-product-compliance
Lightning Source LLC
Chambersburg PA
CBHW061007260726
48661CB00005B/2099